Be The Cat

A Marketing Book With Claws

Blaine Parker

with Fancy Footwork by
The Fabulous Honey Parker

DEDICATION

To my avenger of the Gods and the judge of words. With you, all of this is possible.

TABLE OF CATENTS

INTRODUCTION

"Thou art the Great Cat, the avenger of the Gods, and the judge of words, and the president of the sovereign chiefs and the governor of the holy Circle; thou art indeed...the Great Cat."

- Inscription on the Royal Tombs at Thebes

Welcome to the Power of Cats.

Historically iconic.

Endlessly on YouTube.

And a living, breathing parallel to the Power of Brand.

Why Cats and Brand?

Because it just makes sense.

And who doesn't love yet another cat book?

It also turns our own cat, his litter box and his scratch pads, into a tax deduction.

(If you're an IRS auditor reading this, that's just a joke. We have not and never will attempt to deduct the cat. Unless we take him to dinner to discuss the book. Which is unlikely. Have you ever tried to take a cat to a nice restaurant? No fun for you. And it annoys the cat.)

Cats are a good parallel for brand because of what they represent.

For example, cats are polarizing.

One can love them. Or hate them.

Are you a cat lover or a cat hater?

Equally as polarizing as the cat is a potent brand. See also: Apple Computer.

Apple users love their computers and mobile devices.

There's also a Facebook page called I Hate Apple.

Many computer users, especially some

genuine geeks, hate the Apple product.

Are you an Apple lover or an Apple hater?

Additionally, cats all look similar. Yet each has its own, distinctive characteristics.

So, too, with brand. Even in the same category, no two brands are identical.

Take automotive brands.

Each has unique and distinctive characteristics. Every vehicle will get you from point A to point B.

But the Jeep and Ferrari brands each exhibit unique and distinctive characteristics.

Each makes you feel something very different.

Are you a Jeep or a Ferrari? Or something else?

Cats can also make you happy.

Just like McDonalds or Motel 6.

McDonalds wants you lovin' it.

Motel 6 leaves the light on for you.

Of course, McDonald's or Motel 6 might not speak to you.

Much like my wife's old Persian cat, Baron Yosef, your brand might be Ruth's Chris Steakhouse or Ritz Carlton Hotels.

Before Yosef moved on at age 21, he was the avenger of the Gods.

He was the judge of words.

He was the president of the sovereign chiefs and the governor of the holy Circle.

He indeed was the Great Cat.

And he knew it.

So, how about you?

You need to be the cat.

Are you the great cat?

1. A WORK OF GENIUS

*"The smallest feline is a
masterpiece."*

- Leonardo da Vinci

Signor da Vinci was a brand genius.

Even though he knew nothing of brand as
we know it.

And his observation of scale and
masterpiece is important.

The smallest feline is a masterpiece?

So it should be with the smallest brand.

Which flies in the face of a common belief:

brand is only for big, hulking, lion-sized businesses.

As the great da Vinci himself might have said, *al contrario*.

The smaller you are, the more important brand is.

Because the smaller you are, the more difficult it is to be seen.

The smaller you are, the more of an impression you need to make.

For the smallest feline, think: kitten.

How much fun is a kitten?

How much does it make you feel?

Take my wife, a successful professional and entrepreneur. She completely understands how to be steely in the office.

But take her into Petco, hand her a kitten, and all rational thought goes flying out the doggie door.

She becomes a grinning, wide-eyed puddle of "Can We Take It Home?"

Welcome to the masterpiece of the smallest feline.

It suspends rational thought and becomes magnetic.

As it should be with even the smallest brand.

But what is the smallest brand?

Probably a sole proprietor using social media.

There is no storefront. No inventory. No production. No employees.

Just one man or woman, an internet connection, and the digits.

Take, for example, a struggling comedy writer named Justin Halpern.

He had recently moved back into his dad's house.

That should offer some idea about his success at comedy writing up to that point.

Then, with the prodding of a friend, he opened a Twitter account.

He could have tweeted under the Twitter handle @JustinHalpern.

He could have tweeted all the funny things that came to his mind.

And remained just one of millions of twittering voices in the microblogosphere.

Instead, he tweeted under the handle @ShitMyDadSays.

Every single tweet was another crazy, profane, hilarious thing his dad said.

His twitstream became a sensation.

There came a best-selling book.

Then a network sitcom that won a People's Choice Award.

Then another book.

Which is being developed into a TV series by an important Hollywood comedy producer who is himself a potent small brand.

As one of the smallest of brands, @ShitMyDadSays is a masterpiece.

Yes, it's profane. You may not be.

Yes, it's a brand for a writer. You may sell widgets.

Yes, it's comedy. There may be nothing funny about your family-owned funeral parlour.

None of this changes the value of the brand lesson.

The smallest possible brand — one man with no product but his words — thrives. Why? Because he is focused and makes his customers feel one very specific thing.

Yes, a tiny brand that evokes a strong emotion.

There are plenty of established writers in Hollywood who can't get work.

We know a fabulous, Oscar-winning screenwriter who continually has to work at getting work.

But a tiny, unknown brand developed by one man alone in a room with his words became a sensation.

The smallest masterpiece of a brand.

Like Mr. Halpern, the essence of your business

might not be the emotional equivalent of a kitten.

Nonetheless, your business may also be very, very small.

So be it.

What matters here is essence.

What is the essence of your business?

How does it make people feel?

And how do you focus that essence into a well-crafted, masterpiece of brand?

We are not as lucky as the cat.

We have to work at this.

But da Vinci had it right for both the smallest felines and the smallest brands: masterpiece, indeed.

Be the masterful cat.

2. SPIRIT

"I love cats because I enjoy my home; and little by little, they become its visible soul."

- Jean Cocteau

The visible soul.

Wow.

That's a lot of weight to heap on the cat.

Except that the cat doesn't care.

He'll just ignorantly shoulder the burden that Monsieur Cocteau has heaped upon him.

And the parallel with brand is this: The

Brand becomes the visible soul of the business.

Yes, yes, I know. You're a bean counter. You're a literalist. You're a cold-hearted number cruncher who maintains that a business doesn't have a soul.

You're in the wrong book.

But if you stick around, you might learn something.

No, technically, a business does not have a soul.

But a business is about people. And you'll like this, because you can't argue with law. The law has bestowed personhood upon corporations.

So, if a business is about people, and the law lets us treat a business as a person in court, then the business has a soul.

Deal with it.

Now, as we were saying before we got side tracked by bean counters, the brand is the visible soul of a company.

There may be no more powerful example of

this than Apple Computer.

If you're one of the Apple haters from the last chapter, please bear with me. You don't have to buy their products. You merely have to recognize the truth of the example.

Apple Computer is a unique and distinctive company.

Industrial design is enormously important at Apple.

So is a seamless hardware/software integration.

Apple products must be life-changing.

These qualities are absolutely the visible soul of the late Steve Jobs.

He was a unique and distinctive individual.

He was utterly obsessed with good design.

He believed that for computers to run properly, they required a holistic hardware/software architecture.

He believed that done properly, computers could change lives.

Steve Jobs was a driven, fanatical, acid-dropping hippy who went to India seeking true enlightenment.

Then he started a computer company.

Apple Computer is a brand that could only have been built by that driven, fanatical, enlightenment-seeking, acid-dropping hippy.

The Apple brand is the visible soul of Steve Jobs.

In many ways, the Microsoft brand is the visible soul of Bill Gates. He's much less of an artist and much more of an engineer than Jobs was.

The Wendy's Hamburgers brand is very much the visible soul of Dave Thomas. Dave was committed to a high quality product, good value, and exceptional customer service.

The Virgin Air brand is the visible soul of Sir Richard Branson. Sir Richard is an entrepreneurial whiz, an adventurer, and something of an eccentric. These qualities are reflected in his airlines.

It's possible to go on.

But you probably get the point.

Monsieur Cocteau's cats are the visible soul of his home.

Your brand is the visible soul of your business.

The business is you.

Be the business cat.

BLAINE PARKER

3. EVERYONE'S FAVORITE SUBJECT

"Cats...are flatterers."

- Walter Savage Landor

I hate to break this to you.

It's not all about you.

Your brand is about exactly one person: your core customer.

Cats are flatterers?

So is your brand.

It flatters your customer.

Cats flatter you into believing they love

you.

They make you want to pet them. Feed them. Play with them. Will your estate to them.

The truth?

The cat's primary interest is herself.

That's not to say her flattery is insincere. She may indeed have a bond with you.

But we project much more onto the cat than the cat is capable of being.

That's part and parcel of the cat's brand. "Love me. I do."

Let's go back to Apple Computer, since it's a brand that is almost as ubiquitous as cats.

SIDEBAR: There are roughly 400 million iOS devices and 100 million McIntosh computers worldwide. That's 500 million total units. The world's cat population is estimated at 500-600 million. Conceivably, every cat could have an Apple device. Even though they lack opposable thumbs.

Apple has always been very good at flattering you into desiring its products.

You may have resisted.

But you may also have resisted getting a cat. No matter how much of a wet puddle of "Can we take it home?" you've become.

Back in the 1990s, Apple came back from the brink of disaster when Steve Jobs returned to run the company.

At the time, Apple ran a high-profile ad campaign that never showed you a computer.

It was the "Think Different" campaign.

It flattered you into aligning yourself with geniuses. Albert Einstein. John Lennon. Frank Lloyd Wright. Amelia Earhart.

It flattered you into believing that by using the Mac, you were a potential genius. One of the "crazy ones," the "misfits," the "rebels."

This Jobsian philosophy of crazy, misfit rebellion is deep at the core of the Apple brand.

And the advertising said, Come on in, the water's great!

Think about the first iPod advertising. It was all about people expressing themselves by dancing to music on the iPod.

It made you want an iPod. Even if you can't dance. Even if you have only one leg and use a walker.

Because it was about you and the joy of the music.

It flattered you into joining the party.

Go to another high profile American brand, one that people are surprised to find out is worth two-billion dollars: Motel 6.

Motel 6 is very good at flattering you into believing they love you.

What's that? You doubt they love you?

But for over a quarter century they've been saying, "We'll leave the light on for you."

Who does that?

Your mother? Your spouse?

The light is always left on by people who care you're out there and want you home safe.

It's not a sophisticated brand.

It's not Apple Computer.

It's a budget motel chain.

It's a simple, homespun brand that promises one thing: the lowest priced motel room of any national chain.

But low price is not the brand.

The brand is how Motel 6 makes you feel.

It's how they flatter you into believing they care.

Now, understand that we're not talking empty flattery.

For a brand to actually work, especially over decades like both Apple and Motel 6, the flattery requires an element of sincerity.

You really have to care about the customer and convey what's truly in it for him.

Imagine if Motel 6 was insincere. What if

their facilities were not as functional and clean as they promise? If their employees were nasty and their rooms were overpriced?

The brand would not work.

One reason the Motel 6 brand does work is because they do their best to live up to the promise of the flattery.

One reason the Apple brand works is they do their best to live up to the flattery.

There are genuine high-tech computer geeks who love Apple products. The products are simple. They're user-friendly. They're elegant.

All these things prove Apple cares about the customer experience.

And, as one software company CEO said to us, he switched to Apple because "They just work."

Deceptively simple praise, indeed.

Like the cat, your brand must flatter your customer.

But the flattery must come from a place of

caring about the customer experience.

Empty flattery fails.

Sincere flattery sells.

Be the flattering cat.

4. WHAT'S IN A NAME?

"The Naming of Cats is a difficult matter..."

- T.S. Eliot

My wife did not have to name her first cat. He came to her with a name and a pedigree.

Who else would come up with a name like Baron Yosef but a breeder of pedigreed Persian cats?

And one simply does not rename a pedigreed cat.

Just as one does not rename Jeep.

Which is now owned largely by Fiat.

Which also owns Ferrari.

Now there's an example of some seriously different cats of automotive branding—all in the same family.

However, one must typically name both one's cat and one's business.

And if you think naming a cat is difficult?

Try naming a business.

Especially an advertising agency or a high-tech company. (We've done both.)

When my wife and I brought home the first cat we acquired together, naming him took a day.

We eventually settled on one of the first names we came up with: Miles Davis.

After all, an odd black cat with a raspy voice?

Figuring that one out is almost like shooting fish in a barrel.

Though less messy.

SIDEBAR: If you have lived under a rock your whole life, or are simply far too young to know, Miles Davis was one of the 20th century's most iconic and influential jazz musicians. He was a trumpeter. And a very funky cat. With a raspy voice. Who, by his own account, "changed music five or six times." Start with his quadruple platinum album *Kinda Blue*. Take it from there.

Naming our first company together took much longer than a day.

If you go by the deceptively simple directive that your name must (a) sound good, (b) resonate with your core customer, and (c) convey the essence of your brand, it seems simple.

Then you sit down with a pen and paper.

You find it would be far simpler to gouge out your own eyes with a grapefruit spoon.

Or to get your cat to do your taxes.

To get to a name, we thought about what we mean as a business.

My wife, The Fabulous Honey Parker, spent over two decades working in some of the world's biggest ad agencies.

I am a student of the men whose names were on the doors of some of the world's biggest ad agencies.

I had also spent two decades applying their thinking to small business marketing.

We have both had enormous successes in Direct Response advertising.

(DR is any advertising with an offer and a call to action. Example: "Get this luxury, mink-lined cat box for 50% off. Call now.")

We also didn't want to focus on the DR model. It's almost always based on selling a lot of product quickly.

Instead, we wanted to focus on advertising from the brand up.

When you start with a solid brand, all your

advertising becomes much easier.

And it leads to long-term health.

Because you're focusing on the core of your business and why it matters to your core customer.

Direct Response typically creates a flash in the pan.

Which leads to cycles of feast or famine.

We don't like feast or famine cycling. We prefer long, steady cycling that builds.

We finally settled on a name.

Slow Burn.

But not Slow Burn Advertising.

Why?

Advertising is purely about creating advertisements.

We want to be able to look at a client's big picture.

We want to look not only at advertising, but at everything else.

Like the advertiser's brand.

Like the customer experience.

Like the way they're answering the phone.

Advertising is built atop a house of cards.

You can do everything right in the advertising.

But if the cards beneath it aren't assembled well, you're screwed.

If employees answer phone calls incorrectly, the advertising doesn't matter.

If the customer experience doesn't match the promise of the advertising, the advertising doesn't matter.

If the name of the company is all wrong, the advertising doesn't matter.

Advertising is task specific.

Advertising is an offer to sell.

Marketing is a general effort.

Marketing is holistic.

Being marketing consultants lets us say, "We can't advertise you like Tiffany. Your business looks like the inside of a cat box. And a plastic one. Not one that's lined with mink."

Our brand name became Slow Burn Marketing.

We offer big brand thinking for small business marketing.

It took us a long time to get to that name.

But it was worth it.

Because people Get It.

Instantly.

Another example…

An estate planning law firm came to us for help.

They wanted to re-brand.

Like so many law firms, the lawyer's name was on the door.

And that's it.

Jane Doe, Attorney At Law.

It doesn't explain what they do besides "law."

It has no emotional hook.

It isn't evocative.

It doesn't make the core customer feel anything.

It pretty much leaves one with a question mark.

You certainly know what Gloria Allred does. She has a distinctive personal brand.

She rights grievous wrongs done to regular women on the national stage.

And she does it on TV wearing a red dress and red lipstick, her black hair coiffed confidently. Her steely gaze pierces you to your very soul. Despite not even knowing what the case is about, you feel your own guilt.

You may not like Ms. Allred.

Like the cat, she is a polarizing force.

And like da Vinci's smallest feline, she is also a masterpiece.

The Gloria Allred brand is rock solid.

You also probably have no idea what her law firm is named.

Her law firm's brand is arguably weak. She herself is the strong brand. She is the cat that people pay attention to.

Our lawyer client is not famous.

She is not a relentless self promoter.

She is never on TV.

The only thing she does is the best possible job she can do.

And that job is helping people of a certain age protect their assets for the long haul.

She helps them avoid being ruined by healthcare costs.

She helps them protect their assets from avaricious predators.

She helps them take advantage of benefits they are owed.

In short: she helps seniors have the edge in

retirement and beyond.

Her new business name?

It took a while.

But it was worth it.

She is now Senior Edge Legal.

Tag line: It's your turn.

Know what?

Her core customer Gets It.

They know what her law firm does.

She's also approaching retirement herself.

Know which law firm is easier to sell?

A firm with merely her name on the door?

Or a firm named Senior Edge Legal?

Yet another example…

United Eye Care Specialists came to us for advice.

One of the first things we said is, "You're not United Eye Care Specialists."

Yep. That's what we said.

"United Eye Care Specialists is the name of a big, corporate operation with antiseptic hallways.

"You don't even have a hallway.

"You're a rural eye clinic with one doctor.

"United Eye Care Specialists is also an impersonal, uncaring brand.

"You care more than anyone we've ever met.

"United Eye Care Specialists would speak in jargon and legalese.

"You speak to people like a regular guy and you give it to them straight."

The new name?

Dr. Sam's Eye Care.

Tag line: Straight Talk. Better Vision.

Guess how much better people feel about Dr. Sam's Eye Care.

Guess who has actually achieved local

celebrity status by being on the radio as Dr. Sam.

Guess who increased their patient base and expanded their business.

Hint: not United Eye Care Specialists.

The straight-talking, Dr. Sam's Eye Care brand connects with people. It makes them feel something. It reflects what happens inside that clinic.

The name also didn't come in a flash.

It took time, it took thought, and it was one of several possible names.

T.S. Eliot was absolutely right.

The naming of cats is a difficult matter.

You have to live with both the cat and the cat's name.

Possibly for 21 years, as The Fabulous Honey Parker did with Yosef.

Equally difficult is determining the name of your brand.

It takes work.

It rarely happens in a flash.

That's one of the reasons this chapter is over twice as long as any of the chapters before it.

But when you do the work and you get the name right, great things happen.

Your brand, like your cat, makes sense to the world.

Be the named cat.

BLAINE PARKER

5. IT ALL STARTS AT THE TOP

"Happy owner, happy cat. Indifferent owner, reclusive cat."

- Chinese Proverb

We've got friends who are serious dog people.

Their dogs are always around.

They bound, they bark, they show you their toys. (The dogs. Not our friends.)

It was probably a year before we realized our friends also had a cat.

They are largely indifferent to the cat.

The cat is largely indifferent to them.

And to the dogs.

And to visitors.

Going back to Jean Cocteau, our friend's cat is in no way the visible soul of their home.

Contrast that with Miles Davis. (Our cat. Not the jazz trumpeter.)

Like us, Miles is a happy, sociable animal. He is more than happy to come out and play with strangers.

As a metaphor for brand, our friends' cat is typical of so many businesses we've all patronized.

There is no room for you or me, the customers.

The salespeople don't go out of their way to serve you. They hide and skulk. They'd rather not have anything to do with you.

Like our friends' cat.

I can't even remember her name.

But people remember Miles' name.

Many folks are attracted to him.

More than a few like to wind him up and watch him go. (Which often results in some minor bloodshed or snagged clothing.)

Like a good brand, Miles Davis (the cat) is engaging, evocative and attractive.

He is magnetic.

People want to take him home.

A brand starts at the top.

We've already talked about big brands and their founders. How their founders inform the brand culture.

Like Apple Computer.

Wendy's Hamburgers.

Virgin Air.

Even Gloria Allred and Justin Halpern, who aren't classic examples of brand.

But are owners of valuable brands.

None of these brand owners are indifferent.

From Justin to Jobs, their brands are happy and thriving and live to serve.

Yes, Steve Jobs and Dave Thomas may have moved on.

But their philosophies and cultures survive and thrive. They are highly visible. Their brands are protected by people who care and carry the flame.

There is an enormous national company that's probably worth billions.

Their brand is crap.

They are largely indifferent to the customer. The service stinks. They're expensive.

I used to spend about $2,000 a year with them.

I won't do business with them anymore.

Some people must. In certain markets, this company has a virtual monopoly.

But it's plainly evident that they have indifferent leadership.

And their cat is indifferent. So to speak.

Another example...

Have you been to Sears lately?

It's not like going to Sears 40 years ago.

Sears & Roebuck used to be a thriving department store chain.

The brand used to be the visible soul of Richard Warren Sears and Alvah Curtis Roebuck.

The company had a reputation for high-quality products and high customer satisfaction.

Today, Sears struggles to be profitable.

One gets a sense of a bottom-line oriented leadership. It feels like there's a lack of focus on the brand and an indifference to the customer experience.

It seems as though the cat doesn't care.

I really feel for everyone in Sears' top leadership. They have a very difficult row to hoe. (Hoeing a row is, historically speaking, an apt metaphor. Sears was originally started to serve rural farmers.)

Contrast Sears with a department store that's almost as old with about one third the revenues: Nordstrom.

Nordstrom thrives and is profitable. Even in the recession that continues as of this writing.

Nordstrom is fabled for their customer service and high quality product lines.

Up until a few years ago, this was the *entire* text of the Nordstrom employee handbook:

WELCOME TO NORDSTROM

We're glad to have you with our Company. Our number one goal is to provide outstanding customer service. Set both your personal and professional goals high. We have great confidence in your ability to achieve them.

NORDSTROM RULES: RULE #1: USE BEST JUDGMENT IN ALL SITUATIONS. THERE WILL BE NO ADDITIONAL RULES.

Please feel free to ask your department manager, store manager, or division general manager any question at any time.

Wow.

Talk about a happy cat owner making for a happy cat.

This is a pithy, potent and empowering treatise from the cat owner. It gives the employee cat a lot of credit and a lot of license.

This handbook was printed on a single 5 x 8 inch card.

There is now a somewhat longer handbook with various rules and regulations.

But the original card is still distributed with the book.

The Nordstrom brand is much more

focused and evocative than the Sears brand. It is much more of a masterpiece feline.

Sears is somewhat more like a litter of rabbits.

Sears has so many divisions and subsidiaries and holdings that you probably can't identify them all.

Sears is certainly trying.

Who knows what will happen to their cat.

Nordstrom is one of those Great Cats. The brand is the visible soul. It is a flatterer.

Once upon a time, I worked for a high-end technology retailer with two stores. I was a commissioned salesman. The business was very much the product of a happy cat owner, so to speak.

Technically speaking, the owner's business wasn't as well branded as it could have been.

But he made up for what he lacked in a formal brand image.

He infused the business with his verve, enthusiasm and expertise.

He infused this spirit in his staff.

We delivered it to the customer.

It was largely successful.

His business survived in a highly competitive environment. It lasted for decades after his competitors went under.

Customers would visit us after going to superstore-competitors and become gleeful.

They got truly friendly, informed, enthusiastic and professional service—and they also got a better price.

One year, the owner wasn't so happy.

Business was down.

So he didn't deliver the Christmas bonuses.

The bonuses were always modest. But they had also been thoughtful and personal.

And when they didn't appear that year, he also never communicated about it.

Because of his indifference, the staff was left to wonder.

It created low-key animosity.

It bred its own kind of indifference.

Within a year, several long-time employees simply left.

He had created a tragic brand mistake that didn't actually affect the way the brand looks.

But it hurt the way the brand behaved.

He survived it.

But it had to have made things harder.

For instance, he wasn't at all happy when yours truly left.

I'd decided to move on to a better, more suitable position in marketing.

The first words out of his mouth were angry and all about him.

When he finally extended congratulations, they were tepid at best.

His brand started at the top, and started well.

He was a happy cat owner who suddenly,

briefly became an indifferent cat owner.

And he paid the price.

The brand starts at the top.

It filters its way down to the employees.

And the emotions at the top are contagious.

We won't talk about the other brand where I worked that was ruled by arrogance, fear and intimidation.

Nor the stellar brand that went public and became a product of managerial ignorance and a bean-counter's poverty mentality.

You can imagine.

Let's focus instead on your furry little brand.

What about it?

Is your brand a happy cat or an indifferent cat?

Or something else?

Be the happy cat.

6. GO BIG OR GO HOME

"A cat is a lion in a jungle of small bushes."

- Indian Saying

And really, who can argue with that?

It's about as enlightened an observation about cats as one would expect from the land of enlightenment.

It's also an absolute truth about brands.

We have a mantra that we always offer people. We tell them: Brand Big.

Everything is relative.

And you're only as big as you act.

If you present yourself as a lion in your local jungle of small bushes, guess what.

You're the lion.

Contrast that with your competitor who has no idea what he is.

Unbranded businesses with no identity presenting themselves inconsistently are businesses adrift.

The local cat is king of the small jungle.

Here's an example.

We have a client who specializes in dental practice management consultation.

Sexy, right?

The company name was Innovative Practice Solutions.

Also (ahem) sexy.

They came to us for rebranding. The reason was two-fold.

One, there was another business with the

same name in a nearby state. They wanted to get the monkey of brand confusion off their backs.

Two, the existing brand, such as it was, seemed very girly.

The brand colors were very soft and pastel.

And their image system included a monarch butterfly emerging from a cocoon.

Since the goal of the business was to improve a dental practice, the idea of the image was to symbolize change.

The male consultants did not enjoy the branding.

They were uncomfortable handing out their business cards.

They felt like they were representing some kind of a feminine product.

After much discussion and debate, they chose a name that had come to us in a fit of outlandish thinking.

The new company name is Salt Dental Practice Management.

Yes, Salt.

Salt takes good things and makes them better.

Salt is an essential element for survival.

And, for a business that serves a high percentage of Indian clients, the meaning of salt runs deep.

One of Gandhi's earliest acts of defiance against British rule was the Salt March. It was a protest against the tax on salt. Protesters defied the law. Many produced their own salt from the ocean. 80,000 Indians were jailed.

So, Salt is significant for everyone.

More so for some.

Next came a new logo, and a website explaining Salt DPM.

It used colors that made both the men and the women comfortable.

The web copy made it clear that this was an effort to make good practices into great practices.

It made a sincere effort to flatter the dentist. (There's that flattering cat again.)

The overall brand attitude became bigger and bolder.

And something interesting happened.

Within six months of rebranding, they had doubled their client base.

Their consultants were re-energized.

That's also not the really interesting part.

The really interesting part was: they became a lion in a jungle of small bushes.

Salt is a small operation with only a few account reps.

At an annual national convention, they were being approached by reps from the biggest of their competitors.

We're talking the national and even international consultancies with deep, deep pockets and 20 times the accounts.

These reps were saying how much they loved Salt's new brand and the attitude that went with it.

Salt DPM might be the smallest of felines.

But they are a flatterer.

And they have become a lion in a jungle of small bushes.

How small is your jungle and how big can you brand?

As large as a lion?

Be the big cat.

7. THE STRAIGHT DOPE

"A cat has absolute emotional honesty..."

- Ernest Hemingway

When you get right down to it, the cat gives it to you straight.

You know pretty much how the cat feels about you at any given moment.

The cat is incapable of pretending to be something it's not.

Know what else has to be emotionally honest?

That's right.

Your brand.

So often, starry-eyed, well-intentioned business owners try to build brands around the wrong emotional core.

If you're a small business owner, especially a sole proprietor, you have to go to work every day and be that brand.

If the brand isn't emotionally honest, it prints.

People can feel it.

There's a big urban mattress retailer whose brand is built around him being the crazy guy with the insane low prices.

The brand reflects the guy's true persona.

And for decades, he's been the crazy mattress guy with the insane low prices.

Then, there's another mattress guy.

He goes on the radio and he tries to be the crazy mattress guy with insane low prices.

And it is so painfully obvious that this in no way reflects any aspect of his personality.

He can't pull it off.

It's a lame attempt at being a me-too brand.

It also doesn't match his billboards, which have a nursery rhyme character on them.

It's a dishonest brand from a guy who's fooling himself.

He'd be much happier and more successful with a brand that reflects the guy he actually is.

Another example…

There's a local plumbing brand based on a superhero and his sidekick.

The advertising is grating.

There's nothing honest about it.

It is merely clever.

I couldn't even tell you the name of the business.

And it probably doesn't even matter.

Because you probably have one just like it in your market.

I know that I've had one in other markets I've lived in. I know because once upon a time, I helped create such a brand.

Yes, even marketing professionals are not immune from creating annoying, dishonest brands.

Most marketing professionals, at some point in their careers, suffer from cleveritis.

It's a disease that pushes one to be clever without actually being relevant.

In Big Advertising Agencies, cleveritis often results in what Big Time Ad Pros call Borrowed Interest.

Borrowed Interest is when you borrow an interesting idea from somewhere.

Then, you paste it on your own advertising, even though it has no actual relevance.

For example: "I know, let's sell our cars using clowns!"

Result: "We're not clowning around when

it's time to sell you a car!" HONK HONK!

Unless it's a car dealership actually run by clowns, this doesn't make a lot of sense.

Let's take it a step further.

Instead of just clever advertising, let's put the Borrowed Interest onto the branding.

"I know, let's be the Clown Car Dealer!"

And the business becomes Chuckle's Auto Sales.

The cars are kept under a big top.

There are lots of balloons.

And the salesmen all wear red noses and floppy shoes.

Sound like fun for you, the car buyer?

If not, imagine how much fun it would be to work there.

How much would you enjoy going to work every day?

Especially if you had to maintain the artifice of being a clown.

Unless you actually ARE a clown.

If you're a former professional clown, and it's deep in your blood, and you can figure out a way to parlay that into a car dealer brand, well…

I don't envy you.

I don't know that it's going to resonate with a majority of the car buying public.

But if you're honestly a clown, if it's more than just artifice, have at it.

As for the plumbing superhero, it's easy to see where that brand comes from.

You come swooping in at any hour to right the wrongs of errant plumbing.

And if you're committed to that cartoon superhero brand, and you buy plenty of media, and you keep putting it out there every day, you can make it work.

It's just an awful lot of money and time spent promoting a brand based on a contrivance.

And who is ever going to stop you on the

street and say to you, "Hey, YOU'RE the superhero plumber guy! Wow!"

Because that guy doesn't exist.

Contrast that with Dr. Sam's Eye Care.

After only a few months of being on the radio, Dr. Sam was handing some outgoing mail to a postman.

The postman looked at the envelopes and said, "Dr. Sam's Eye Care? Are YOU Dr. Sam? Wow!"

An honest brand marketed well can create celebrity.

Take Mike Diamond.

He's a plumbing guy in Los Angeles.

He's the guy with the "on-time, good smelling plumbers."

Mike is in all the Mike Diamond Plumbing advertising. And he promises that when you call, your plumber will be on time and smell good.

And if that doesn't happen, he offers you

compensation.

It's an easy brand to live up to because it's simple, honest and real.

Mike Diamond's brand makes him the Great Cat of Plumbing in Los Angeles.

Since Mike himself promises something so simple and attainable, he seems like the Masterpiece of the Smallest Feline.

Even though his company is quite large.

And the brand of Mike is the visible soul of the business.

The brand is the Flattering Cat.

It flatters you with the idea that you have standards.

The naming of the cat here doesn't seem to have been a difficult matter.

Mike Diamond used his own name.

Which, frankly, isn't very imaginative.

It didn't take a lot of work to get there.

But there's something to be said for

longevity. His name has been on the business since he was a one-man shop over 30 years ago. So there's some heritage involved.

You don't necessarily want to give up equity like that.

According to Mike Diamond's website, *The Los Angeles Business Journal* has a name for him: "L.A.'s Most Famous Plumber."

There's a book from J.D. Power & Associates called *Satisfaction: How Every Great Company Listens to the Voice of the Customer*.

Mike Diamond Plumbing is profiled in that book.

What if Mike Diamond had decided to brand himself like a cartoon superhero?

He could have done it.

But would it have been as successful?

The superhero brand is a contrivance.

The man as the brand is Hemingway's emotionally honest cat.

And he doesn't have to go to work every

day trying to be something he isn't.

Can you turn your brand into the Great Cat by being the emotionally honest cat?

That doesn't mean you have to actually put your own name on the brand and be in your advertising.

It also doesn't mean you can't be a superhero.

But do you really want to be someone else's cartoon?

Be the emotionally honest cat.

8. BETTER LIVING THROUGH CUSTOMER CHEMISTRY

"By associating with the cat, one only risks becoming richer."

- Sidonie Gabrielle

Sidonie Gabrielle was an interesting cat.

She was a firebrand of a French woman born in the 1800s.

She was an author, a performer, and a famous bisexual.

As they said repeatedly in an infamous episode of *Seinfeld*, not that there's anything wrong with that.

But it certainly led Ms. Gabrielle to a very, very high brand profile in a much less progressive time.

Sidonie Gabrielle was known better as Colette.

Which is a much better name for both a brand and a cat, IMHO.

And Colette's observation about associating with the cat making one richer should be taken to heart.

We've applied our branding methodology to many clients.

By and large, they've become richer.

And not just richer monetarily.

We did a review of what our clients have accomplished after working on their branding with us.

We realized they typically double something.

Some have doubled their revenues.

Others have doubled their client base.

Still others have doubled the fun they're having at work.

Some have doubled the appreciation they get from their customers.

Brand has indeed made each one of our clients better, happier and richer.

Starting a business?

We heartily encourage a deep brand soul searching before launching oneself at an unsuspecting public.

Have an existing business?

We recommend deep introspection about the existing brand — if there even is one.

Sole proprietor? Social media maven?

Ditto.

We live in an overcommunicated culture.

Your customer is bombarded with an estimated 3,000 advertising messages per day.

The higher your profile, the more you cut through.

The more cat-influenced your brand, the more people pay attention.

And care.

"For all your marketing needs" is not a line we would ever, ever use in our own marketing.

Because we are Big Agency Thinking For Small Business Marketing.

And no big agency has ever unleashed any brand while using the word "needs."

Motel 6: for all your cheap lodging needs.

McDonalds: for all your fast food hamburger needs.

Southwest Airlines: for all your budget air travel needs.

BMW: for all your luxury driving needs.

Nike: for all your athletic clothing needs.

Nope.

None of 'em.

"We'll leave the light on for you."

"I'm lovin' it."

"You are now free to move about the country."

"The ultimate driving machine."

"Just do it."

All of those businesses are richer for their Great Cat brands.

They each dig deep into the psyche of their core customer.

They determine the intersection between the chemistry of their company and the chemistry of their core customer.

They understand how and why they do what they do, and how and why it matters to the core customer.

And they find a way to express it emotionally and honestly.

And by doing so, they enrich the lives of their customers.

Colette was right.

By associating with the cat, one only risks becoming richer.

By branding with cues from the cat, your business only risks becoming richer.

And for the customer who risks associating with your brand?

The same.

Go forth.

Brand big.

May the cat be with you.

Be the rich cat.

AFTERWORD

Meow.

ABOUT THE AUTHOR

Blaine Parker is a national-award winning, ROI-generating advertising Creative Director and copywriter. He helps his much smarter wife, the Fabulous Honey Parker, run Slow Burn Marketing from high atop a defensible mountain ridge outside beautiful Park City, Utah. Slow Burn specializes in big brand thinking for small business marketing. Their client roster spans from New Hampshire to San Diego to Toronto to Calgary to the Philippines. (Yes, outsourcing can work both ways.)

www.ingramcontent.com/pod-product-compliance
Lightning Source LLC
Chambersburg PA
CBHW060642210326
41520CB00010B/1704